THE BOOK OF UNCOMMON EXPLANATIONS

The Interesting Stories Behind Things and Exposing How Things Work

Kate Callaghan

COPY RIGHT

ACREST PRESS

Contents

Introduction

Since I was a child, I've been an avid lover of facts. As far back as I can remember, I found myself drawn to books and resources filled with knowledge and information. While other kids were immersed in fantastical tales of adventure and mystery, I was engrossed in the encyclopedias, almanacs, and reference books that lined my shelves. I was on a quest to absorb facts about the world around me.

As I leafed through the pages of fact-filled volumes, I began to notice something remarkable happening. Facts weren't just random details; they were the threads that wove together the fabric of understanding. They connected the dots, revealing a beautiful tapestry of knowledge that spanned across countless disciplines.

My love for facts wasn't about memorizing trivia; it was about building a solid foundation of understanding. These books of facts became my portals to various worlds of knowledge. They allowed me to explore history, science, art, geography, and more. With each new fact I encountered, my curiosity was piqued, and I yearned to delve deeper into the subject matter. This thirst for knowledge became my lifelong pursuit.

Today, I can proudly say that my fascination with facts has led to a robust understanding of a myriad of subjects. I am confident in my ability to engage in conversations with individuals from diverse disciplines, thanks to the rich tapestry of facts that I've woven throughout the years. Whether it's discussing the intricacies of quantum mechanics, the masterpieces of classical art, the historical turning points that shaped our world, or the marvels of the natural world, facts have been my trusted companions.

In this book, I aim to share with you the profound influence that facts have had on my life. I will take you on a journey through the incredible world of facts, highlighting their power to inform, inspire, and connect us with the wealth of human knowledge. Together, we will explore the role of facts in shaping our understanding of the universe, our history, our culture, and our future.

So, join me in this exploration of the facts that have molded my understanding of the world. Let's embark on a quest to unravel the mysteries, embrace the wonders, and appreciate the profound insights that facts offer us. For, in the realm of facts, we discover not just knowledge but the foundation upon which we can build our collective understanding and appreciation of the world we inhabit.

Why are the keys on Keyboard not in alphabetical order?

The arrangement of keys on modern keyboards deviates from alphabetical order due to historical and practical considerations. The lineage of contemporary keyboards can be traced back to the typewriter, a device first conceived by Christopher Latham Sholes in the 1860s. Sholes encountered a significant challenge with the early typewriters: their mechanical arms, responsible for striking the paper with characters, often became entangled and jammed when users typed rapidly.

To address this issue, Sholes implemented a strategic redesign of the key layout, aiming to slow down typing speed and diminish the chances of mechanical arm jams. This restructuring gave birth to the QWERTY keyboard layout.

The QWERTY layout, which continues to be the predominant choice for keyboards today, was deliberately crafted to position the most frequently used letters in less accessible locations, thus impeding typing speed. This design was influenced by the prevalence of letter combinations in the English language, all in the pursuit of minimizing the occurrence of mechanical arm jams.

Despite the development of alternative keyboard layouts over time, such as the Dvorak Simplified Keyboard and the Colemak keyboard, the QWERTY layout has endured as the preferred choice. Its enduring popularity can be attributed to its familiarity among users and widespread acceptance. Additionally, the prospect of transitioning to a different key layout presents a significant inconvenience, necessitating users to relearn typing skills.

In recent years, these alternative keyboard layouts have emerged, offering promises of increased efficiency and ergonomic benefits compared to the QWERTY layout. Nonetheless, their adoption remains limited due to the substantial learning curve associated with switching to a new keyboard configuration.

What is Blood Rain?

Blood rain, also referred to as "red rain," is a meteorological occurrence in which rainfall takes on hues of red, pink, or brown. Its name is derived from its resemblance to the color of blood.

The causes of this phenomenon vary depending on specific circumstances. In certain instances, it can be attributed to the presence of airborne particles like dust or sand, which can impart a reddish tint to the rainwater. This occurrence is particularly prevalent in arid regions where strong winds can lift substantial quantities of dust and sand into the atmosphere.

Another potential factor behind blood rain is the existence of algae or other microorganisms within the water. Some types of algae are known to produce pigments that can give water a reddish or pinkish hue. If these organisms are present in significant concentrations, they can cause the rainwater to take on a red appearance.

In some cases, blood rain has been associated with volcanic activity. During a volcanic eruption, ash and particles can ascend to great heights in the atmosphere, where they can be disseminated over wide areas by prevailing winds. If these particles become intermingled with rain clouds, they can mix with the rainwater and impart a red or brown coloration.

In summary, blood rain is a relatively infrequent meteorological event, typically carrying no significant health risks to humans or animals. Nonetheless, it is a visually striking and at times disconcerting phenomenon that has intrigued and inspired speculation for centuries.

What are Skin Banks?

Skin banks are vital necessities in the medical world! Consider a location where they gather, jazz up, and store donated human skin. Why, you might ask? It's for really vital things like assisting burn patients or assisting people with skin graft procedures and other reconstructive magic.

So, how do they get this skin? It's not like they just scoop it up off the sidewalk! Nope, they do a mini-surgery where they snag a tiny piece of skin from a generous donor's body. But wait, there's a catch – donors have to pass a specialized screening and testing to make sure there are no sneaky diseases or infections lurking around. Safety first!

Once they've got that precious skin, it's off to the lab for a spa day. They clean it up and get it all dolled up for storage. And where do they store it? In a super-sterile, chilly wonderland to keep it from going all floppy. They freeze it in a special solution that's like a magical elixir for skin, keeping it fresh and strong. And get this – it can hang out there for up to five years before it's called into action!

Now, when it's time for action, they thaw it out and prep it for its big moment. The skin can be useful in various ways, like a temporary patch for burn victims or even as a full-time replacement for skin that's gone MIA.

How do Submarines navigate underwater?

Ahoy there, underwater explorers! Submarines are like the stealthy ninjas of the deep sea, and they've got some pretty cool tricks up their sleeves for navigating and communicating.

First off, when it comes to finding their way in the watery depths, submarines have a trio of trusty companions. There's the "Inertial Navigation System," which is like a fancy fitness tracker for the sub. It uses accelerometers and gyroscopes to measure how fast the sub is moving and which way it's turning. With that info, it can figure out exactly where it is and how fast it's going – super handy!

Then, there's "Sonar" – think of it as the submarine's echolocation system. It sends out sound waves that bounce off stuff in the water, like other vessels, underwater hills, or even curious marine critters. By listening to the echoes, the sub can tell what's around, just like how a bat knows where it's flying in the dark.

And who could forget the good old "GPS"? Yep, submarines can use it too, but here's the catch – they have to be near the surface to catch those signals from the GPS satellites up in the sky. Surface sneak peek, anyone?

Now, staying in touch with the surface world can be a bit tricky when you're hiding beneath the waves. But submarines have got that covered too! They've got "buoyant antennas" that they can pop out through a special tube in their hull. These antennas float up to the surface and play catch with radio signals, talking to other vessels or stations on shore.

And if that's not cool enough, they can also chat using sound, just like underwater telephones. These acoustic signals let them have secret conversations while staying incognito.

So, there you have it, the underwater adventures of submarines – navigating and communicating like the stealthy sea pros they are!

What are contact Lenses made of?

Contact lenses come in three main flavors, each with its own unique ingredients:

1. **Soft Contacts:** These are like the marshmallows of contact lenses. They're made from a flexible, water-loving material called hydrogel. Imagine them as sponges that happily soak up water to stay soft and comfy. Depending on the brand and type, their water content can range from around 38% to a whopping 75% by weight. This built-in hydration helps oxygen pass through the lenses, keeping your corneas happy and healthy while you rock your contacts.

2. **Gas Permeable Contacts (GP or RGP):** These lenses are the tough cookies of the bunch. Unlike their soft cousins, they're rigid or hard. But don't let that fool you! They're still "gas permeable," meaning they let oxygen flow through to your corneas. However, GPs don't rely on water to get the job done. Instead, their microscopic pores do the heavy lifting, making sure your eyes get the oxygen they need without all that extra H2O.

3. **Hybrid Contacts:** Picture these as the best of both worlds. Hybrid lenses have a rock-solid, gas-permeable center (the optical zone) for crisp vision and durability. But they're not all business! Around the edges, they sport a cozy, soft contact lens material for a snug and comfy fit. It's like having the durability of a GP lens and the comfort of a soft one, all in a single lens.

So, whether you're into soft and squishy, sturdy and gas-permeable, or the hybrid combo deal, there's a contact lens to match your style and comfort. Your eyes, your choice!

How Electric Eels Shock

Electric eels, those underwater shockers of the animal kingdom, have a fascinating way of generating electricity.

They possess special cells called electrocytes, neatly stacked up in organs known as electroplax. Now, when an electric eel decides it's time for some shock therapy, it takes a deep breath – not to calm down but to oxygenate these electrolytes.

Once primed, the electric eel sends out a series of electrical pulses that trigger the electrocytes to release their stored electrical charge. Imagine it as a lightning bolt in the watery world!

The result? An electric discharge with some serious voltage, reaching up to a shocking 600 volts in some species. This electric firepower isn't just for show; it helps them stun prey and send a jolt to any predator that's getting too close for comfort.

So, it's all about these electrolytes and their electrifying potential, making electric eels the underwater electricians of the animal kingdom!

Why do Military Aircraft often fly in formation?

Well, there are some pretty cool reasons!

Tactical Twirls: First off, flying in formation is like a secret weapon during combat. These aircraft become best buddies up there, chatting, knowing what's happening around them, and pulling off some seriously cool maneuvers. It's all about teamwork, baby!

Buddy System: Formation flying isn't just about looking cool; it's about having each other's backs. Imagine having your wingman right there, ready to zoom in if you need help. It's like having a superhero sidekick but with jet engines. Together, they can spot threats, dodge danger, and keep each other safe.

Fuel-Saving Stunts: Oh, and here's a nifty trick – flying close together can actually save fuel. It's like carpooling but in the sky. The planes reduce drag and use the air to their advantage. So, they can stay in the air longer, perfect for those long-haul missions.

Top Gun Training: Formation flying isn't just for show; it's a must-learn skill for military pilots. They practice it to perfection, making sure they can stay close, communicate like champs, and move as one unit. Think of it as the ultimate aerial ballet, where every move is synchronized.

Showtime Spectacle: And when military planes rock the skies in formation during airshows or special events, it's more than just a show. It's a statement of strength, unity, and national pride. It's like fireworks in the daytime, showing off their power and teamwork to the world.

But remember, while it's awesome, formation flying is no joke. It takes mega training, mad skills, and safety rules galore to keep pilots and planes out of harm's way. It's like a high-flying art that combines precision and power!

Litmus Paper

Litmus paper is like the mood ring of the chemistry world! It's this fantastic paper that helps you figure out whether a substance is acidic or alkaline, and it's loaded with natural dyes from cool lichens, like the rockstar Roccella tinctoria.

So, we've got two showstoppers: blue litmus paper and red litmus paper. They each start with their own swagger.

Blue Litmus Paper: Think of it as your "bluesy" buddy. In its natural state, it's rocking that deep blue look. But if it bumps into something acidic, like lemon juice or vinegar, it's party time! The acid hands over hydrogen ions, and voila, the blue paper goes all red. It's like it's singing a different tune!

Red Litmus Paper: Now, meet the "red hot" sibling. It's red from the get-go. But when it meets an alkaline (basic) substance, like when baking soda gets in the mix, things heat up. The alkaline stuff snatches hydrogen ions from the paper, and bam, the red paper turns blue. It's like a color-changing magic trick!

But here's the deal: litmus paper isn't about getting all nerdy with pH numbers. It's more like a quick test to see if something is acidic (red alert!) or alkaline (blue sky ahead!). Simple, right?

So, whether you're in a lab, a classroom, or a doctor's office, litmus paper is like the fun, easy way to add a splash of color to your chemistry adventures. It's all about vibes and chemistry magic!

Why do Wine glasses have stems?

The birthplace of the stemmed glass takes us on a time-travel adventure to Venice, the bustling hub of glassmaking, back in the 1400s. It all started with a nod to chalices used for religious ceremonies, and wine, well, it was sipped from all sorts of vessels like wood, leather, pewter, or clay. Stemware was basically the shy wallflower at the party. But around 1450, the game changed with the invention of cristallo glass, a game-changer that added a touch of elegance to glassware, especially with its crystal-clear charm.

Fast forward to the late 18th century, and stemware finally took the spotlight. The glassware business was booming, and the stars of the show were those graceful, stemmed glasses.

Now, let's talk wine etiquette. The golden rule? Keep that wine at the perfect temperature from the moment it's stored to the moment it meets your lips. You see, our hands are like cozy little furnaces, and the stem of the glass is our lifesaver. It lets us hold the glass without turning it into a wine sauna. Why's that a big deal? Because when you touch the bowl instead of the stem, your hand's warmth can sneak into the glass and start playing with the wine's temperature. Nobody wants the alcohol to overshadow those delicate flavors.

But that's not all! Holding the glass by the stem also keeps those pesky fingerprints and smudges at bay. Wine is a work of art, and you wouldn't want grease marks stealing the spotlight.

And speaking of wine magic, there's that all-important swirl. It's not just for show; it's like a gentle wake-up call for the wine's aromas. With the stem as your partner in crime, swirling becomes a breeze. You can admire the wine's color dance and take it all in. Just remember, if you're new to swirling, take it slow – we wouldn't want any precious drops going overboard.

So, the next time you're sipping from a stemmed glass, you're not just enjoying wine – you're dancing through centuries of history and tradition. Cheers to that!

"Sugar-free", "No sugar added" and "Unsweetened" Explained

Navigating food labels can feel like deciphering a secret code! You might have noticed terms like "sugar-free," "no sugar added," and "unsweetened" on different products and wondered if they're all the same. Well, let's unravel this sweet mystery!

Sugar-Free: Imagine this as a sugar-free oasis. When a product says "sugar-free," it's shouting from the rooftops that there's no added sugar or sugar-based sweeteners. But hold on, that doesn't mean it's tasteless. Sometimes, they sneak in sugar alcohols or artificial sweeteners to keep things sweet without the sugar.

No Sugar Added: This one's like the middle ground. "No sugar added" means they didn't sprinkle extra sugar in during the making. But there's a catch: it might still have natural sugars, like the sweetness found in fruits or dairy. So, take a peek at the nutrition facts to see if there's sugar hiding in plain sight.

Unsweetened: Think of this as the no-nonsense approach. When something's "unsweetened," it means they didn't add any sweeteners, whether natural or artificial. It's like the food or drink is saying, "I'm going au naturel." But remember, it could still have natural sugars depending on what's inside.

Now, when you're on a sugar-watching mission, reading those labels like a detective is key. Check the ingredients list to spot any undercover sweeteners. And always keep your personal dietary needs and taste buds in mind.

So, there you have it – the sweet story behind "sugar-free," "no sugar added," and "unsweetened." It's all about knowing what you're really getting when you dive into that deliciousness!

What is Gesture Recognition Technology and How Does It Work?

Gesture recognition technology is all about understanding the moves you make, like a digital dance partner. So, what's the deal with it, and how does it groove to your gestures?

Imagine you're waving your hand in a funky pattern in front of your device, and boom, your favorite app launches. That's gesture recognition at work! It's like your device is reading your dance moves, but in the digital world.

Now, here's the cool part: gesture recognition is part of the "touchless" club. Unlike your trusty touchscreen, which needs your fingertips, gesture recognition lets you control stuff without a touch. Think of voice-controlled smart speakers like Google Home or Amazon Alexa – you chat, and they obey. But gesture recognition adds a fun twist by reading your moves.

Here's the secret sauce: your device has sensors or cameras watching your every move. They're like the audience at your digital dance-off. When they see a move that matches a command, they go, "Aha!" and make things happen. It could be unlocking your device, launching apps, adjusting the volume – you name it!

So, whether you're waving your hand, making a peace sign, or doing the robot dance, gesture recognition is like your tech-savvy partner that follows your lead without a touch. It's like magic, but with digital moves!

What is the importance of the Foundation in building construction?

The importance of a solid foundation in building construction cannot be overstated. Here are several key reasons why a well-designed and strong foundation is essential:

1. **Structural Integrity:** The foundation forms the base upon which the entire building rests. It distributes the weight of the structure evenly, ensuring stability. This structural integrity is vital to withstand various forces, including the building's own weight, environmental factors, and potential seismic activity.

2. **Stability**: A strong foundation ensures the building remains stable and level. It prevents tilting, shifting, or sinking, which can occur due to changes in the soil beneath the structure. Stability is critical for the safety and functionality of the building.

3. **Prevents Settlement:** Properly designed foundations help prevent settlement or sinking of the building over time. Settlement can lead to structural damage, cracks in walls and floors, and costly repairs. A solid foundation minimizes these risks.

4. **Longevity:** A well-constructed foundation contributes to the long-term durability of the building. It helps protect against moisture, soil erosion, and other factors that can lead to the deterioration of the structure. A strong foundation can extend the lifespan of the building, reducing maintenance and repair costs.

5. **Building Code Compliance:** Building codes and regulations mandate specific standards for foundations to ensure safety and structural integrity. Compliance with these codes is essential to obtain necessary permits and certifications. A properly designed and constructed foundation ensures adherence to these regulations.

In summary, the foundation is the cornerstone of a building's structural integrity and longevity. It provides stability, prevents settlement, and ensures compliance with building codes. A strong and well-designed foundation is essential for the safety, durability, and functionality of any construction project.

Soaps and Detergents, the Scientific explanation of how they Work.

Well, these cleaning agents are made of special molecules called surfactants. Surf-what? Surfactants have a head that's best buds with water (hydrophilic), and a tail that's like a grease-loving detective (hydrophobic).

When these surfactant molecules dive into the laundry battle, their heads stay in the water while their tails cozy up to the grease and dirt. It's like they're throwing a secret grease party!

But here's where the magic happens: the head group's love for water is so strong that it starts tugging the grease away from the surface. They form a detergent force field around the grease, breaking it into tiny pieces.

And guess what? These mini-grease bits get washed away by the water, leaving your clothes sparkling clean. It's like a grease disappearing act!

But wait, there's more! Our surfactants also make water act super wet. You know how water blobs like to stick together and stay put? Well, surfactants step in and break up this water gang, making it spread out and get all cozy with your clothes.

So, next time you see soap or detergent in action, remember they're like the cool heroes of cleaning, breaking down grease, and making water do the wet work. Cleaning has never been this fun!

Why does my stomach make funny sounds when I am hungry?

Your stomach has a secret language, and it loves to talk when you're hungry! That rumbling and growling you hear is called "borborygmi" (try saying that three times fast).

Here's the scoop: when you go without food for a bit, your stomach and intestines kick into action. They do this cool thing called the "migrating motor complex" (MMC), which is like a digestive dance routine.

During this dance, your tummy muscles contract and move stuff around, like gas, fluids, and digestive juices. It's like a digestive traffic jam! When these contractions mix with air and liquid, they create the symphony of growling sounds you hear.

So, your stomach growls when you're hungry because it's getting ready for the mealtime tango. But remember, borborygmi can also happen for other reasons, like gas or the movement of, well, you know what. So, embrace your stomach's secret language—it's just doing its thing!

What causes Bones to make popping sounds?

Cracking or popping sounds that occur when we crack our knuckles or other joints are fascinating and involve the science of synovial fluid, joint capsules, and dissolved gasses.

Picture this: inside your joints, there are these slick surfaces where bones meet, and they're surrounded by a capsule. This capsule is filled with synovial fluid, which is like a lubricant for your joints. It also has some dissolved gasses chilling out, like oxygen, nitrogen, and carbon dioxide.

Now, when you apply gentle force to your joint, like when you crack your knuckles, the capsule starts to stretch. But there's a limit to how much it can stretch, and one factor is the volume of the joint. That volume is determined by how much synovial fluid is inside. But here's where the magic happens: when you stretch the joint, the pressure inside drops just enough for those dissolved gasses to escape from the synovial fluid.

When these gasses pop out of the solution, they create a tiny gas bubble inside the joint. This bubble increases the joint's volume by about 15 to 20 percent and makes a cracking sound in the process. The main gas in this bubble is carbon dioxide.

But here's the kicker: you can't just keep cracking the same joint over and over because those gasses need time to dissolve back into the synovial fluid. So, the next time your joints crack, remember it's like a gas bubble party in there, and science is the DJ!

How do Fireworks get their colors?

Fireworks are like magical bursts of color in the night sky, and they get their vibrant hues through a clever mix of science and art.

Picture a fireworks shell, which is like a fancy container. Inside this container, there are compartments. The bottom one contains black powder, which is like the fuel for the fireworks. It's a mix of potassium nitrate, charcoal, and sulfur.

Now, the real showstoppers are in the top compartment. That's where you find the pyrotechnic stars, and they're like the paint for our fireworks canvas. These stars are made from a fuel that burns and special minerals and metals that bring the colors to life.

Here's the secret recipe for these colorful stars: they have five main ingredients.

1. Fuel to keep them burning.
2. An oxidizer that provides oxygen to make the fuel burn.

3. Color-producing chemicals to give us those stunning hues.

4. A binder to hold everything together.

5. Sometimes, a chlorine donor that adds extra oomph to the colors (though the oxidizer can sometimes do this job).

Now, each color has its own special ingredient. Barium gives us vibrant greens, strontium makes deep reds, copper creates blues, and sodium delivers sunny yellows. If you mix some of these elements, you get even more colors. For example, strontium and sodium together make a brilliant orange, and a combo of titanium, zirconium, and magnesium gives us silvery white.

But it's not just about colors. The gold sparks you see are made from iron filings and bits of charcoal, while those bright flashes and big bangs come from aluminum powder.

So, when you watch fireworks light up the night sky, remember that it's science and a dash of artistry that paint those beautiful, fleeting pictures for us all to enjoy!

Why does the Nose of some people start bleeding at Higher altitude?

Going up to higher altitudes can be quite an adventure, but it can sometimes lead to a peculiar problem: nosebleeds. Let's unravel the mystery of why this happens!

You see, our bodies are used to the air pressure at ground level. As we climb higher, like up a mountain, the atmospheric pressure decreases. It's like the air up there is lighter. But our bodies need some time to adjust to this change in pressure.

Now, here's where the nose comes into play. Inside our noses, there's a soft and sensitive part called the mucosa. It's like the delicate lining of your nasal passages. When you're at higher altitudes, the air is not just lighter; it's also drier. And that dry air can sap the moisture from this sensitive mucosa.

Think of it as your nose getting a little parched, like when you're thirsty. As a result, this inner skin can develop tiny cracks, which, in turn, can lead to nosebleeds. So, when you blow your nose or even just breathe, those tiny cracks can start to bleed.

But don't worry, there's a way to deal with it! If you find yourself with a nosebleed at a higher altitude, try these steps:

1. Sit up straight and tilt your head slightly forward.
2. Pinch the soft part of your nose using your thumb and a finger. This helps put pressure on the bleeding point inside your nose.
3. Breathe through your mouth while your nose is pinched.
4. After about 10 minutes, check if the bleeding has stopped by gently releasing the pressure. If it hasn't stopped, pinch again for another 10 minutes.
5. You can also apply an ice pack to your nose and cheeks. The cold helps narrow your blood vessels and might stop the bleeding.

So, next time you're on a high-altitude adventure and your nose starts to act up, you'll know it's just your body adjusting to the thinner, drier air. Stay hydrated, and you'll be just fine!

How does a Defibrillator work?

A defibrillator is like a conductor for your heart's orchestra, ready to restore harmony when things go awry. It's like a maestro wielding a baton to bring your heart's notes back in tune during cardiac distress.

First, know that there are various types of defibrillators, each with its unique role in the orchestra of life. Whether it's biphasic, monophasic, an automated external defibrillator (AED), or an internal one with or without a pacemaker (AICD), their mission remains the same: to restore the heart's natural rhythm.

Now, visualize this: cardiac arrest is a cacophonous symphony within your heart, with electrical signals playing discordant tunes. This disrupts the flow of vital oxygenated blood throughout your body.

When someone collapses, unresponsive, it's a signal that their heart's ensemble has lost its way. You won't detect their pulse, and they won't draw breath. In these critical moments, they only have a brief window of opportunity.

Enter the defibrillator as the orchestra's conductor. It delivers a precise electrical pulse to the heart's stage, akin to a conductor's baton guiding musicians. This pulse momentarily silences the dissonance within the heart's musicians.

Here's the enchantment: during this brief pause, the heart's musicians regroup and catch their breath. It's like offering them a moment of reflection to regain their harmony and remember how to play in synchrony.

When the defibrillator fulfills its role, the heart returns to its natural rhythm, a harmonious melody known as sinus rhythm. And that's the goal – a heart that beats in perfect cadence, orchestrating the flow of life's vitality to every corner of the body.

So, the next time you witness a defibrillator in action, envision it as a conductor of life's orchestra, restoring the heart's beautiful symphony and allowing the music of life to play on.

What is the concept behind Leap Year?

The concept of a leap year is like a cosmic calendar adjustment. You see, our Earth's journey around the sun takes approximately 365.24219 days, not a neat and tidy 365 days. Those extra fractional days may not seem like much, but over time, they can throw our calendars into chaos.

Picture this: If we stuck strictly to a 365-day calendar, our dates would slowly drift out of sync with the Earth's position in its orbit. Seasons would fall out of place, and we'd be planting crops in the snow and skiing in the sweltering heat.

To keep things in cosmic harmony, the idea of a leap year was born. It's like a cosmic correction tape for our calendars. Here's how it works:

1. Every four years, we add an extra day to the calendar, creating a "leap year." This extra day is February 29th, making that year 366 days long instead of the usual 365.

2. This simple adjustment helps us catch up with the Earth's actual orbit. It ensures that our seasons stay aligned with the calendar, and we don't end up with summer in December.

But wait, there's more to the story. Even our cosmic calendar correction isn't perfect. You see, the leap year system slightly overcompensates for those extra fractions of a day. So, to fine-tune things, there's another rule:

3. Century years (like 1800, 1900, and 2000) aren't leap years, unless they're divisible by 400 (like the year 2000). This rule ensures we don't add too many leap years and keeps our calendar aligned with the solar system.

With these adjustments, we're doing a cosmic dance, keeping our calendars and seasons in sync, one leap year at a time. It's like a little cosmic choreography to make sure our Earth-bound lives stay harmonized with the rhythms of the universe.

How are Pearls formed?

Natural pearls are formed inside oyster shells. Oysters dwell at the sea bottom, keeping their shells tightly closed. Occasionally, tiny particles like grains of sand find their way inside the shell, causing irritation to the oyster. In response, the oyster secretes a substance, similar to what forms its shell, to coat and lessen the irritation caused by the foreign particle. Over time, this grain of sand grows in size as more layers of the coating material accumulate and harden around it. Eventually, it develops into a substantial structure known as a pearl. This pearl can be carefully extracted from the oyster's shell and prepared for various uses.

In the case of cultured pearls, humans play an active role in this process. They deliberately introduce the sand into oysters in controlled environments, such as pearl farms, and monitor the pearl's growth. When the pearl reaches the desired size, it is harvested and prepared for use.

Freshwater pearls generally have a shape resembling small grains of sand, while saltwater pearls and cultured pearls tend to have a rounder appearance.

Why does banging your Elbow give you an Electric Shock?

Ever wondered why hitting your elbow feels like getting a zesty electric shock? Well, stay with me, because the mystery of the "funny bone" is about to be unveiled.

First off, let's debunk the myth – the funny bone isn't really a bone. It's more like a nerve highway, known as the Ulnar Nerve, running from your arm to your hand. Now, here's where the drama unfolds.

Right there at your elbow, there's a little nook called the cubital tunnel. It's where this vulnerable nerve hangs out, with not much protection from the outside world. So, when you accidentally bonk your funny bone on something, that poor, defenseless nerve gets squeezed against the bone. Ouch!

The result? You feel an unexpected surge of pain, like a mini electric shock, shooting down your arm. It's like your body's way of saying, "Hey, that wasn't cool!" The nerve protests loudly, and you're left with that tingling sensation, often described as pins and needles.

But here's the good news – it usually goes away as swiftly as it came. So, fear not, and keep those elbows safe from any humorous encounters!

How does Airbag work in automobiles?

When a car collides with something, it's like hitting the brakes on speed real fast. But here's the secret sauce behind airbags – the unsung hero, the accelerometer. it is like a tiny chip that's all about measuring the forces of acceleration.

Now, when things get intense and the deceleration happens at lightning speed, that trusty accelerometer senses it. But here's the kicker – regular braking won't cut it; it's got to be a real showstopper.

So, our clever accelerometer signals the airbag circuit into action. Think of this as a backstage pass to the airbag's grand entrance. The circuit kicks off by sending an electric current through a heating element, just like the wire in your toaster (but with way more flair).

That heating element ignites a chemical explosive – yes, you read that right! In the old days, it was sodium azide, but nowadays, we've got some new players in town. As this explosive does its thing, it conjures up a massive cloud of friendly gas (usually nitrogen or argon), and this gas is no party crasher; it's here to save the day.

This gas rushes into a snug nylon bag, patiently waiting behind your steering wheel. And when it bursts onto the scene, it's showtime! The bag puffs up and kicks the plastic cover off the steering wheel like a superhero's cape unfurling.

picture yourself in the driver's seat – the car's come to a halt, but you're still moving forward from the impact. You push against this magnificent bag, and it goes, "Whoosh!" The gas inside makes its grand exit through tiny holes around the bag's edges.

By the time the curtain falls on this airbag performance, it's all deflated and back to normal. That's the magic of how these life-saving cushions work!

What causes Red Eyes in Photos?

Ever wondered why photos sometimes give people and animals creepy red eyes? Well, let's dive into this photographic mystery.

The culprit here is none other than the "red-eye effect." It's that common scenario where your subject's eyes seem to turn into fiery red orbs in your photos. So, what's the story?

Here's the scoop: It all goes down when you use a camera flash super close to the lens, especially in dim lighting. Compact cameras are usually the culprits. This pesky effect messes with human and animal eyes alike, especially those with a special feature called the "tapetum lucidum."

Now, what in the world is the tapetum lucidum, you ask? It's like a built-in reflector system in the eyes of many critters. This system is a nifty trick of evolution, usually there to give their light-sensitive retinas a double dose of light by bouncing it back for another round of photoreceptor stimulation. In simpler terms, it's like a natural night vision upgrade.

But when that camera flash pops up close, the tapetum lucidum reflects the light straight back into the camera lens, and boom – you've got those crimson peepers staring back at you in your photos.

So, the next time you're snapping pics in low light with a flash, remember, the tapetum lucidum is the sneaky sidekick behind the red-eye effect.

Why is the Medical symbol a snake on a stick?

The serpent-entwined staff, often referred to as the "Rod of Asclepius," holds a rich history and symbolism in the realm of medicine. This symbol finds its roots in ancient Greek mythology, particularly associated with Asclepius, the Greek god of healing and medicine. Asclepius is often depicted holding this staff, and the snake entwined around it symbolizes rejuvenation and the healing process.

However, a common misconception arises when people confuse this symbol with another one, the Caduceus. The Caduceus features a short staff with two snakes and a winged top. This symbol belongs to Hermes in Greek mythology (known as Mercury in Roman mythology), the messenger of the gods. It signifies various concepts like travel, commerce, and negotiation.

The historical mix-up and misidentification of these symbols can be traced back to around the 1920s when the U.S. Army unintentionally adopted the Caduceus as a symbol for its medical personnel. This choice contributed to some of the confusion regarding the symbolism of medicine.

In summary, the Rod of Asclepius with a single serpent represents medicine and healing, rooted in Greek mythology, while the Caduceus with two snakes and wings is associated with Hermes and conveys different concepts like commerce and communication.

How exactly does the Sun provide us with Vitamin D?

It is a myth that sunlight provides us vitamin D or vitamin D is present in sunlight.

The fact is vitamin D is synthesized in plants, animals and humans in presence of sunlight.

There are two types of vitamin D - vitamin D2 (Ergocalciferol) present in plants including ergot and mushrooms and vitamin D3 (Cholecalciferol) in animals.

Vitamin D2 (Ergocalciferol) and vitamin D3 (Cholecalciferol) are synthesised in presence of ultraviolet light (UV) of sunlight as given below.

In plants, the ergo-calciferol (vitamin D2) is derived from UV irradiation of ergosterol (a kind of sterol present in plants).

In animals and humans, when skin is exposed to sunlight, chole-calciferol (vitamin D3) is produced in skin by UV irradiation of 7-dehydro-cholesterol (a kind of cholesterol present in animals and humans).

Sunlight triggers the first of three chemical reactions that converts an inactive compound in the skin into active vitamin D. Ultraviolet B rays from the sun convert a natural vitamin D precursor present in your skin, 7-dehydrocholesterol, into vitamin D3. This travels to the liver where the addition of oxygen and hydrogen to vitamin D3 changes it into 25-hydroxyvitamin D. Doctors test for this intermediate and still inactive form of vitamin D in blood to determine your vitamin D status. Final activation of 25-hydroxyvitamin D takes place in the kidneys, where more oxygen and hydrogen molecules attach to 25-hydroxyvitamin D and convert it into its active form known as 1,25 dihydroxyvitamin D, or calcitriol.

Why do Pilots wear headphones?

Alright, let's dive into the world of aviation headsets – where serious meets a touch of techy fun!

So, we've got two main players here: the passive noise reduction headsets and the snazzy active noise reduction (ANR) headsets. The passive ones are like those quiet introverts at a party. They snugly seal around your ears and give you that reassuring "shh" without needing any fancy batteries. Simple and reliable – no drama!

Now, the ANR headsets are the cool kids who need some power to show off their noise-cancelling wizardry. But hey, even when they're off duty, they can still pull off a decent hush-hush act. They're like that friend who's the life of the party but can also be chill when needed. Just remember, don't mix up their power sources – it's not like swapping phone chargers!

When you plug in, you've got two choices. Helicopters prefer the "one-plug wonder," where the microphone and headphones share a cozy socket. Airplanes, on the other hand, like to keep things separate – one plug for headphones and one for the microphone. No mix-ups allowed in the cockpit – it's like their own version of "stay in your lane."

Now, the real party happens when you connect to the airplane's audio panel. Think of it as the DJ booth of the skies. It's got an intercom for chitchatting with your fellow flyers and a direct line to air traffic control. Plus, it's eavesdropping on those navigation radios – because who doesn't love a little gossip?

But here's where it gets interesting: you can either go full-on "hot mic" mode, where you're always "live," or you can have a mic with manners. The squelch control is your best friend here – it's like the hush button for those moments when you're not the star of the show. And when you're chatting with air traffic control, just hit that push-to-talk (PTT) switch – it's your golden ticket to cockpit communication!

Why is Salt used to melt ice on the Roads in Winter?

Picture this: a frosty winter's day, and the temperature takes a nosedive to 32 degrees Fahrenheit (0 degrees Celsius). When this happens, ice can start forming, including those treacherous patches on the road.

Now, let's talk about road salt, which plays a crucial role in combating icy roads. Road salt does something pretty clever known as "freezing point depression." This scientific concept involves lowering the freezing point of water.

Here's the deal: When you spread road salt, you're essentially telling water, "Hold off on freezing until it gets much colder!" If you have a 10-percent salt solution, water will resist freezing until it reaches a chilly 20 degrees Fahrenheit (-6 Celsius). And if you kick it up a notch to a 20-percent solution, water will stubbornly refuse to freeze until it's a bone-chilling 2 degrees Fahrenheit (-16 Celsius).

But here's the catch – road salt needs a partner, and that partner is water. If the road is as dry as a desert, tossing salt won't do the trick. That's why you often see those trucks applying a brine solution, which is essentially salt mixed with water.

This dynamic duo gets to work before the icy conditions arrive, ensuring that ice struggles to take hold. It's like a protective shield against winter's frosty grip! Plus, it's a smart move because it means we'll need less road salt later to combat icy roads.

So, there you have it – road salt and freezing point depression, working hand in hand to keep our roads safer during the winter season!

Why sometimes Water freezes instantly with just a shake?

Imagine a bottle of incredibly pure water, so pure that it's like the water's on a quest for its inner zen. This water is so squeaky clean that it doesn't have any of those pesky impurities floating around. Now, usually, when water starts to chill out and get cold, it wants to transform into ice, like a caterpillar turning into a butterfly. But, there's a catch—ice needs a little kickstart, a special spot to begin its ice-making journey. We call this magical spot a "nucleation site."

In typical water, these nucleation sites can be tiny impurities or particles just hanging out, ready to spark the ice-making process. They're like the friendly guides showing water molecules the way to becoming ice.

Now, back to our ultra-pure water. It's got no impurities, no particles, and no tour guides for the ice-transformation adventure. So, the water molecules are all dressed up for the ice ball but have no dance floor to groove on.

When you give that bottle a good shake, it's like sending a shockwave through this calm and pristine water world. A few lucky water molecules seize the opportunity to line up just right and start the crystal party. Once the first ice crystal is formed, it's like a "do not disturb" sign goes up, and all the other water molecules join the ice gang.

The ice crystal starts growing in one direction, and it's like an infectious dance that everyone wants to be a part of. Before you know it, all that pure water has transformed into ice, and you've got yourself a bottle full of frosty wonder.

So, shaking that bottle? It's like giving pure water a little nudge, reminding it that it's okay to embrace its inner ice and join the crystalline party. It's a chilly transformation worth celebrating!

How Do Antiperspirants Work?

Let's dive into the fascinating world of underarm companions: deodorants and antiperspirants.

Picture this – you're getting ready to face the day, and you reach for that trusty product on your bathroom shelf. But, have you ever wondered what sets these two superheroes of freshness apart?

First, meet deodorants. They're like the cool, calm, and collected squad members in the fight against body odor. Deodorants don't mess with your perspiration process; instead, they swoop in with their fragrant charm to tackle any unpleasant smells. It's like sending in the odor-fighting cavalry, and they smell good while doing it!

Now, let's talk about antiperspirants – the guardians of dryness. These bad boys mean business. They don't just combat body odor; they're on a mission to stop sweat dead in its tracks. The secret weapon? Aluminum-based compounds, like aluminum chlorohydrate and aluminum-zirconium tetrachlorohydrex gly. When sweat tries to make its grand entrance, these compounds do a little chemical tango with it.

They mess with the sweat's electrolyte mojo and form a sneaky gel plug right inside your sweat gland's duct. This plug says, "Nope, you're not going anywhere!" It's like putting a "Do Not Enter" sign on the sweat gland's door. The result? Sweat is stopped in its tracks over that 'target' area, leaving you feeling fresh and dry.

But here's the twist – these gel plugs aren't permanent gatekeepers. Over time, your skin peels them away naturally. It's like a slow and subtle eviction notice for the gel plug!

So, in a nutshell, antiperspirants are like the bouncers at the sweaty nightclub – they prevent the sweat glands from throwing a wild party. And to top it off, they add a dash of sweet-smelling fragrance to keep you feeling fabulous.

So, whether you're Team Deodorant or Team Antiperspirant, rest assured that you've got your own fresh army ready to tackle whatever the day throws your way!

What happens if Aircraft Engines fail in Mid-Air?

When an aircraft experiences engine failure, it loses the essential thrust needed to either maintain its current altitude or climb further. However, it's crucial to understand that engine failure does not necessarily translate to a complete loss of control over the aircraft. Skilled pilots can use the flight controls at their disposal, particularly the rudders and ailerons, in an assertive manner to navigate the aircraft to safety.

To compensate for the loss of thrust, airplanes may descend in altitude. They typically operate with a thrust-to-drag ratio of 10:1, meaning they can travel forward for 10 miles for every mile of altitude they lose. Cruising at high altitudes, around 35,000 feet (equivalent to approximately 6 miles), provides aircraft with a substantial buffer of about 60 miles to identify a suitable location for an emergency landing. Handling engine failure becomes more manageable at higher altitudes compared to lower altitudes, such as during takeoff.

Pilots confronted with engine failure must make forced landings on the most favorable surface within their reach. Interestingly, this surface doesn't have to be solid ground; aircraft can also be ditched, which means landing on water or ice, without jeopardizing the safety of passengers.

Aircraft, much like cars with crumple zones, are designed with sacrificial components in their structure that absorb the impact force during a landing in challenging terrains. These components may include the wings, landing gear, and even the lower part of the fuselage.

Why do you get Boogers in your Eyes?

The scientific moniker for those charming eye crusties is "rheum." Sounds quite fancy, right? But what's this rheum made of, you ask? Well, it's a mix of mucus, skin cells, oils, and a touch of dust. The particular brand of rheum that originates in your eyes, dries up, and fashions those delightful eye boogers is aptly named "gound." But you might have heard it referred to as eye sand, eye gunk, sleep dust, sleep sand, or simply "sleep in your eyes." Now, when you're up and about during the day, gound behaves itself and doesn't pose any problems.

You see, your eyes are like little factories churning out mucus all day long. However, they've got a clever system in place. Each time you give those peepers a good blink, a thin curtain of tears washes over them, sweeping away the developing gound before it has a chance to solidify and cause a fuss.

But when it's lights out and your blink-o-meter is on standby, that's when the eye discharge takes center stage. It congregates in the corners of your eyes, sometimes cozying up to your lash line, hence the term "sleep in your eyes."

Now, keep in mind that eye discharge isn't just here to annoy you. It can be a sign of various eye conditions, including the ever-popular conjunctivitis. But that's not all, folks! There's a whole roster of eye infections that can turn your eye discharge into an unruly rebel. These troublemakers include eye herpes (yep, even your eyes can get cold sores), fungal keratitis (a rare but not-so-friendly cornea inflammation), and Acanthamoeba keratitis (a potential vision-taker, usually caused by not-so-stellar contact lens hygiene or daring swims with your contacts on).

Why do drugs come in different forms?

medications are like secret agents on a mission. They need to reach the right destination and perform their special tricks to save the day. Now, if you need a medicine to work its magic in your stomach, it makes perfect sense to send in a tablet straight to the belly, right? It's all about getting cozy with the target organ.

Imagine you have a backstage pass to your body's main attractions: the stomach, intestines, mouth, and even the skin. For these VIP areas, we've got the A-list treatment like orally solvable tablets, ointments, and lotions. You know, the red carpet treatment.

But hold on, what about those organs that are like the VIP lounges you can't just stroll into? We're talking about the heart, brain, small intestine, pancreas, and the blood. Those are the VIP lounges with bouncers at the door. For these exclusive clubs, we've got different routes and special formulas.

Here's the grand plan:

1. The "Wow, we need it right now!" route: Sublingual tablets. When there's an emergency, like a sudden heart attack, you don't have time to wait. Pop one of these, and it's like a superhero rushing in for immediate relief.

2. The "Comfortable and Cost-Effective" route: The oral route. It's like the comfy couch of drug delivery. Tablets, capsules, and syrups – this is where you chill and let the drug slowly do its thing. It's affordable and easy but not without its quirks. Sometimes it may irritate your stomach or take a little longer to kick in.

3. The "Direct Delivery to the Scene" route: Topical. This is like sending in the drug SWAT team. They go straight to the site of action, reducing the risk of side effects elsewhere. But watch out for potential skin irritation, and sometimes, controlling the dosage is like trying to keep a toddler from eating all the cookies.

4. The "Inhalation Magic Show" route: Inhaled medications. It's like the David Blaine of drug delivery. Quick absorption, local and systemic action. But remember, it can have a not-so-pleasant taste or even irritate your mouth. Inhaling substances directly to the

brain is like a bullet train for the drug, super potent and swift. (Ah, smoking, we see you.)

5. The "Direct Injection to the Vein" route: Injections. This is when we get serious. Intravenous, intramuscular, subcutaneous – these guys are the fast-track to action. They're like the drug's private jet, with a direct highway into the system. This is perfect for those hard-to-absorb drugs. But beware, there might be a bit of discomfort and a need for some skilled hands to make the magic happen.

So, my friend, next time you take your medicine, remember it's not just a pill; it's a carefully planned operation with different entry points and strategies to get the job done.

What is the difference between CC and BCC when sending an e-mail?

In today's digital age, email has earned its rightful place as one of the most beloved means of communication, catering to the needs of both small businesses and large corporations. Within the realm of email, two little heroes come into play: Cc (Carbon Copy) and Bcc (Blind Carbon Copy). These trusty features ensure the secure exchange of information via email.

Let's unveil their roles:

Cc (Carbon Copy):

- Cc, standing for Carbon Copy, is your go-to for sending duplicates of an email to various recipients. When using Cc, everyone on the email list can see who else has received the same message.
- It's your choice when you want to send an email without the need for a personal address.

- Cc ensures everyone stays in the loop, even when the email isn't their direct concern.

- Cc is your ally when you anticipate responses from the recipients.

- Consider Cc when you wish to keep others informed about the email's contents.

Bcc (Blind Carbon Copy):

- Bcc, short for Blind Carbon Copy, shares similarities with Cc. It's your ticket to sending multiple copies of an email to various recipients without exposing the recipient list.

- Bcc is your choice for sending emails to a multitude of recipients simultaneously.

- When you're all about privacy and don't want each recipient to peek at other email addresses, Bcc is your sidekick.

- In the grand stage of large businesses, Bcc plays a pivotal role.

- Bcc shines when you're sharing company newsletters while keeping your recipients' email addresses under wraps.

- It's your guardian for maintaining the privacy of recipients, especially when sending emails to unknown individuals.
- Bcc is the messenger for those impersonal emails that don't require responses but deserve attention.

So, in the email universe, Cc and Bcc are the dynamic duo that ensure your messages reach the right eyes without compromising anyone's privacy.

What is Dark Web?

The internet, like an iceberg, has its own hidden depths. It's often described in three layers: the surface web, the deep web, and the dark web.

The Surface Web: Imagine the surface web as the tip of the iceberg, the part visible above the water. This is where search engines like Google do their work. If you can find something with a simple online search, it's part of the surface web.

The Deep Web: Now, let's dive a little deeper. The deep web is like the submerged part of the iceberg. It's the largest layer and remains hidden from the prying eyes of search engines. Your personal emails and plenty of other important, non-public information reside here. To access the deep web, you'll need to know the exact URL of the website you're looking for, along with proper authorization if it's a secured or restricted site. Think government documents, confidential military intel, and more.

The Dark Web: The darkest depths of the iceberg belong to the dark web. Here, websites operate on overlay networks that use the internet but demand special tools, configurations, and often, a secret handshake, so to speak, to access. These sites are not your run-of-the-mill web pages and cannot be discovered using your usual search engines. The dark web is just a tiny part of the deep web, even though some folks mistakenly use the term "deep web" to refer specifically to the dark web.

To journey into the dark web, you need to be equipped with tools like the Tor browser, which is highly popular among its users. These special sites often sport the ".onion" domain. Users who dare to venture here enjoy a cloak of anonymity that's like the web's version of a magic invisibility cloak. With advanced encryption that bounces data through various servers, it's like a high-tech cloak of invisibility for your online activities.

But, there's a catch. The dark web, due to its shroud of secrecy, has become a notorious hub for illegal activities. Think of it as the shadowy underbelly of the internet, where illicit trades like drugs and weapons occur, where the black market thrives, and where fraudsters and miscreants meet. On a lighter note, it's also home to whistleblower sites and places for political discussions.

Still, you'll find a fair share of less savory services and transactions, so tread carefully in these mysterious waters.

Why does Mint have a cooling sensation?

Ever wondered why mint feels so refreshingly cool? Well, that's thanks to menthol, the chilly secret hiding in mint's leaves.

Menthol has a nifty trick up its sleeve – it can cozy up to your skin's cold-sensitive TRPM8 receptors. TRPM8 (which stands for transient receptor potential cation channel, subfamily M, member 8) is like a tiny gatekeeper in your body. When it swings open, it lets sodium and calcium ions flow in, creating an electrical signal that zips down your nerves.

But here's where it gets really cool – TRPM8 isn't just any gatekeeper; it's a temperature-sensitive one. It loves to open up when things get chilly. When you munch on something minty, the menthol you're chomping on convinces TRPM8 to swing wide open. And here's the catch – your body can't really tell the difference between the signal from menthol and the one it sends when it's chilly outside. So, when TRPM8 detects menthol, it sends a signal to your brain that says, "Hey, it's cold in here!"

And that's why minty things feel so delightfully cool. It's a taste of winter in every bite or breath!

Why can't we carry Plants, Seeds and Soil on international flights?

When you're heading to an airport, there are a couple of travel companions that aren't welcome aboard: plants, seeds, and soil. You might wonder why something as innocent as a potted plant or a bag of soil would be on the airport's no-fly list. Well, it's all about keeping our ecosystems and agricultural industries safe and sound.

You see, these green travel buddies can secretly carry harmful pests, diseases, and invasive species that could wreak havoc on the environment and crops of the country you're flying into. These troublemakers can spread like wildfire, and once they're out and about, it's a tough task to put them back in their box.

But the plant-soil combo isn't just a threat to nature; it's also a sneaky foe to the aviation industry. Soil might be harboring organisms that are no friends of aircraft. There could be fungi and bacteria just waiting to munch on metal parts, causing corrosion and damage. And those friendly little plants? They could be rolling out the red carpet for insects and birds that like to play near runways and even flirt with aircraft engines – not something you want in an airport's dating scene!

That's why most countries have strict rules and regulations about bringing plants and soil on board. You'll need proper permits and inspections to make sure your leafy or earthy companions aren't hiding any unwanted stowaways. So, next time you're thinking about taking your garden on a plane ride, remember that airports have a green thumb for security, and it's all about keeping things safe and smooth for everyone.

Meaning of the network alphabets?

When you rev up your smartphone's mobile data for some internet action, you might notice a little alphabet soup popping up on your screen. G, E, H, H+, LTE, 3G, 4G, 5G – what's the deal with all these letters? Well, they're like speed indicators for your mobile connection, and they're here to tell you just how fast you can zoom through the internet highway.

Let's break it down:

G: This stands for GPRS, and it's like the grandma of mobile data. It's super slow and uses the old-school GSM network (that's 2G in tech lingo).

E: E is an upgrade from G and is known as EDGE. It's a bit faster but still chugs along on the old GSM network. Think of it as 2.5G.

3G: Ah, here we go, the third generation! It's called UMTS, and it's speedier than its predecessors, leaving 2G in the dust.

H and H+: These are all about HSPA and HSPA+. They're zippier and make use of the UMTS network. H is faster than 3G, and H+ is even faster than H. They're like 3.5G.

4G: Welcome to the fourth generation, or LTE (Long-Term Evolution). This is where things start getting seriously fast.

5G: The new kid on the block. It's the fifth generation, and it's here to replace 4G. With major upgrades in speed, coverage, and reliability, it's like the Usain Bolt of mobile networks.

So next time you see these letters, know that they're just giving you a heads-up on how quickly you can surf the web, from the leisurely stroll of G to the lightning-fast sprint of 5G!

What's the Difference Between a Memoir, a Biography, and an Autobiography?

Life stories come in three distinct flavors: biography, autobiography, and memoir. Each one serves up a unique narrative style.

Biography: This is like the full scoop about someone's life, but with a twist – it's penned by someone else. Picture it as a non-fiction account of a person's journey. The author isn't the star; they're just telling the story of the star. You'll find all the important life events, birthplace info, education bits, career highlights, and juicy relationship tidbits.

Autobiography: In this version, the star of the show is also the author. It's their life, their words. Autobiographies are where folks spill the beans about their own adventures, often in the first-person narrative. It's a way to share their experiences and achievements, and these gems are typically written when they've got a few tales to tell.

Memoir: Memoir, derived from the French word "mémoire," which means memory, is like the warm and fuzzy version of an autobiography. Sure, it's the author's life story, but it's less about raw facts and more about feelings. Memoirs are all about making an emotional connection. The author dives deep into their personal experiences, sharing intimate stories from their journey through life.

So, whether you're in the mood for the whole life enchilada (biography), a first-person adventure (autobiography), or an emotional rollercoaster (memoir), there's a life story format for every taste.

When it comes to Books and Movies, what's a Prequel, Sequel, and Spinoff?

In the realm of books and movies, sequels, prequels, and spinoffs are like the follow-up acts to an original work. They're like the encore performances in the world of storytelling, and each has its unique flavor:

Sequel: Imagine this as the "next chapter" in the original story. A sequel picks up where the original left off, continuing the adventure with the same characters and themes. It's like a new episode in your favorite TV show, following the established plotlines or delving into new ones. Sequels can either hop right from where we left off or take us on a time-traveling journey to explore what's next.

For example: "Harry Potter and the Chamber of Secrets" continues the wizarding journey from "Harry Potter and the Philosopher's Stone."

Prequel: Picture this as a peek into the past. A prequel ventures into the backstory of the characters or events that happened before the original story. It's like uncovering the history of your favorite hero or understanding the events that set the stage for the main plot. Prequels add depth and context to the original narrative.

For example: "The Hobbit" sets the stage for the epic events in "The Lord of the Rings" trilogy.

Spinoff: Think of this as a new adventure in the same universe. A spinoff unfolds in the world created by the original work but shifts the spotlight to different characters or events. It's like exploring a different corner of the same magical land or meeting entirely new folks who share the same backdrop. Spinoffs can be their own independent tales or connect to the original storyline.

For example: "Fantastic Beasts and Where to Find Them" transports us to the "Harry Potter" universe but focuses on Newt Scamander's escapades in New York City.

In both books and movies, these storytelling techniques allow creators to expand on beloved tales. They offer fresh perspectives on characters, events, and worlds, and they open up new avenues for storytelling. But, of course, they come with a bit of risk, as fans often have high expectations. The key is to tread carefully and approach these new adventures with respect for the original work while injecting them with creativity and fresh ideas.

What is Pegasus?

Pegasus, developed by the Israeli company NSO Group, is like a digital spy in the world of technology. It's a tool designed to sneak into and monitor the devices of specific individuals, including smartphones and other mobile gadgets. This software is mainly sold to governments and law enforcement agencies for their intelligence and investigative purposes.

Here's how Pegasus works its digital magic: It looks for weak spots in the target device's operating system, sort of like finding secret doors into a castle. Once inside, it gains access to the device's treasure trove of data and communications. It can eavesdrop on a variety of activities like call logs, texts, emails, and all sorts of messages. Plus, it can grab location info, contact lists, and other personal details.

But Pegasus has a few more tricks up its virtual sleeve. It can activate the device's camera and microphone, essentially turning it into an undercover agent. It can capture audio and video of the surroundings without the user even suspecting a thing.

One of the most controversial aspects of Pegasus is its ability to sneak in without any user interaction, using something called "zero-click" exploits. This means that just receiving a message or call can be all it takes for Pegasus to slither in and install itself on the device. This makes it incredibly hard for the target to spot or prevent the spyware from setting up shop.

The use of Pegasus and similar spyware has sparked a lot of debate. There are worries about potential misuse and privacy violations, as well as concerns about the lack of transparency and oversight when it's used by governments and law enforcement agencies. It's a digital frontier where secrecy and surveillance collide.

What is Cache data and How does it work?

Cache data is like your device's secret weapon for faster performance. It's the stuff it keeps hidden away to make your online experiences snappier. Let's dive into how it works:

Every time you visit a website or use an app, your device saves a little piece of that site or app in its cache. It's like a quick-access storage area where your device keeps the things it thinks you'll want to use again. This makes your life easier because the next time you visit the same place, it can load up much faster.

So, when you ask your device for something – like a web page or a cat video – it first checks its cache to see if it already has it stored. If it finds what you're looking for in the cache, great! It can serve it up super fast, way quicker than downloading it from the internet or some faraway server.

Think of it like having a secret stash of snacks right next to your couch. You don't need to run to the kitchen (the internet) to get your chips; you've got them right there. It's handy and quick!

But, as with any secret stash, it can get a bit cluttered. Cache data takes up space, and too much clutter can slow down your device. So, it's a good idea to give your device a little spring cleaning every now and then by clearing out the cache. This frees up space and ensures your device keeps performing at its best.

In a nutshell, cache data is like your device's shortcut to faster loading times. It keeps a hidden reserve of frequently used stuff so you don't have to wait for it to download from the web every time. A tidy cache is a happy cache!

Does the Human body produce Electricity?

Absolutely, your body has a real spark of brilliance when it comes to electricity! This phenomenon, known as "bioelectrogenesis," is pretty electrifying.

At the heart of this zappy business are special cells called "neurons." These guys are like the electrical engineers of your body. When it's time to send a message, they get to work. Here's how it all goes down:

1. **Ion Dance:** Neurons use a neat trick involving ions (charged particles) to create electrical signals. They've got these channels in their membranes, and when it's time to send a message, they open up.

2. **Charge Shuffle:** When the channels open, positively charged ions rush in, while negatively charged ions head out. This creates a charge difference across the neuron's membrane. Think of it like a battery, but in living color!

3. **Action Time**: Once this charge difference reaches a certain level (we call it a "membrane potential"), it's go-time. An "action potential" is triggered – it's like a lightning bolt, a super-fast change in charge that travels along the neuron.

This whole process is how your body sends electrical messages. It's not just your neurons that are electrifying, though! Your muscles and heart cells also do their own dance with ions to make things move and beat. So, electricity isn't just for your gadgets; it's what keeps you going too!

All in all, it's an intricate and dazzling system that shows just how amazing the human body truly is.

What's the difference between a MAC address and IP address?

Absolutely! MAC and IP addresses are like digital name tags for devices in a computer network, and each serves its own unique purpose.

MAC Address (Media Access Control):
Think of a MAC address as the device's DNA – it's unique, permanent, and determined by the device's manufacturer. This 12-digit hexadecimal code is assigned to the network interface (like your Wi-Fi or Ethernet card) of your device.

MAC addresses are used primarily for local network communications. When your device wants to chat with another device within your home or local area network, it uses MAC addresses. It's like a private conversation where devices recognize each other by their MAC addresses. Your router, for instance, uses MAC addresses to decide who gets to join the Wi-Fi party.

IP Address (Internet Protocol):

IP addresses are more like postal addresses in the digital world. They identify your device's location on a broader network, whether that's your local network or the vast internet. Unlike MAC addresses, IP addresses can change depending on your network and location.

There are two flavors of IP addresses: IPv4 (32-bit) and IPv6 (128-bit). IPv4 is like the classic postal code, but we're running out of those, so IPv6 is like a super-sized version that's been introduced to ensure everyone gets a unique address.

So, while MAC addresses are for private, local communication, IP addresses are like the public addresses for devices on the internet, helping them find their way around the vast digital world.

In a nutshell, MAC addresses are for recognizing devices in your home or local network, and IP addresses are like global postal codes that help devices communicate with the wider world.

How does Active Noise Canceling Headphones work?

Noise-canceling headphones are like your personal sound bodyguards, shielding your ears from the chaos of the outside world. Here's a breakdown of how they do this technological magic:

1. **Microphone:** These headphones come with microphones, sometimes even multiple ones, to pick up the sounds from your surroundings. Think of them as the ears of your headphones.

2. **Electronic Wizardry:** The microphone(s) pass these sounds over to some serious electronic processing power right inside your headphones. Here, it's time to get technical. This processing brain analyzes the incoming sounds and starts cooking up something special.

3. **Anti-Noise Signal:** What comes out of this audio kitchen is an "anti-noise" signal. This signal is like an acoustic ninja that's the exact opposite of the unwanted

noise. It's as if it's saying, "You make noise? I'll make silence."

4. Let the Show Begin: This anti-noise signal is now played through the headphones' speakers. It joins the original sound from your music or audio source and works its magic. Imagine it as the noise-canceling superhero swooping in to defeat the villainous outside noise.

5. User Bliss: What reaches your ears is this beautiful blend of your audio and the anti-noise signal. The result? Unwanted noise is either gone or seriously muted, and you can immerse yourself in your audio without interruptions.

Keep in mind that this is called "active noise-cancellation" because it's actively combating the unwanted noise in real-time. These headphones excel at reducing continuous sounds like the drone of an airplane engine, the rumble of a subway, or the whirring of office chatter. However, they might not be as effective against abrupt, high-pitched noises like sirens or alarms.

Whether you're on a plane, train, in a bustling office, or just craving some peace, noise-canceling headphones are your quiet companions, helping you find your auditory happy place.

How does Self balancing Scooter work?

Absolutely, let's dive into the science of those cool self-balancing scooters, often affectionately called hoverboards, even though they don't quite hover:

1. Sensors: These nifty devices come equipped with gyroscopic sensors. There are usually two sensors—one for each footpad. These sensors are like your scooter's internal detectives. They constantly monitor your center of gravity, detecting any subtle shifts as you lean forward, backward, left, or right.

2. Motors: The scooter has two wheels, and each one has its own motor. These motors can spin independently. When you lean forward, both motors rev up to propel you forward. When you lean back, they slow down to send you in reverse. It's all about balance and counterbalance.

3. Control System: Now, the brain behind the operation is the control system. It processes the data from the gyroscopic sensors and decides how fast each motor should spin to keep you upright and moving in the direction you want. It's like your personal acrobat, making sure you don't tumble.

4. Battery: All this electronic magic needs power, and that's where the rechargeable battery comes in. It's the energy source that keeps the motors running and the control system doing its thing.

So, here's the dance: When you step onto the scooter, the gyroscopic sensors detect your weight and the subtlest movements. The control system immediately calculates what to do. If you lean forward, the sensors pick that up and tell the motors to start spinning faster, propelling you forward. Leaning back? Motors slow down, and you move backward. Want to turn? Shift your weight to one side, and the motors adjust their speeds to make the turn.

It's all a delicate symphony of sensors, motors, and algorithms working together to give you that smooth, self-balancing ride. Just remember, while these scooters make it look easy, it does take some practice to master the art of riding one without any wobbles!

What is E-Bomb?

Electromagnetic bombs, also known as EMP (Electromagnetic Pulse) bombs, are specialized weapons designed to release an intense burst of electromagnetic radiation. This burst of electromagnetic energy can inflict damage upon or even destroy electronic devices. The fundamental concept behind electromagnetic bombs involves generating a brief yet potent electromagnetic field that induces an electrical voltage in conductive materials.

These EMP weapons can be delivered through various means, including missiles, aircraft, or even handheld devices. When the bomb is detonated, it emits a short-lived but powerful burst of electromagnetic energy that affects all electronic devices within its range.

The working principle of electromagnetic bombs is rooted in electromagnetic induction. When a magnetic field undergoes change, it generates an electric field, and conversely, when an electric field changes, it creates a magnetic field. Electromagnetic bombs function by producing a rapidly changing magnetic field, which, in turn, induces an electric field in nearby conductive materials, like wires, circuits, or antennas. This induction can result in electrical currents flowing through the material, potentially leading to damage or destruction.

The impact of an electromagnetic bomb can vary, depending on factors such as the pulse's strength, the distance from the detonation, and the susceptibility of the electronic devices in the affected area. Devices with long wires or antennas are particularly vulnerable. This includes critical infrastructure systems like power grids, communication networks, and transportation systems. An EMP bomb could potentially disrupt or disable these systems, causing significant chaos and disruption on a wide scale.

Conclusion

In this compendium of facts, we've embarked on a journey through a realm of knowledge, discovering the incredible, the curious, and the thought-provoking. From the depths of science to the heights of human achievement, we've delved into a world of facts that expand our horizons and remind us of the sheer wonder of the universe.

In concluding our exploration of this book of facts, it's important to remember that the pursuit of knowledge is an endless adventure. The facts we've encountered are but a small fraction of the vast universe of information that awaits our discovery. Each fact is a stepping stone, inviting us to take the next leap into the unknown.

The beauty of facts lies not only in the knowledge they provide but also in their ability to inspire curiosity and wonder. They fuel our imagination, challenge our preconceptions, and encourage us to question the world around us.

As we close this chapter, let us carry with us the realization that facts are more than mere details; they are the building blocks of understanding, empathy, and innovation. In a world filled with uncertainty, facts offer us a solid foundation upon which we can construct a better future.

So, let us remain curious, let us continue to explore, and let us never cease our pursuit of facts, for they are the keys to unlocking the mysteries of the universe and the potential within ourselves. The journey of discovery is infinite, and the wonder of facts is eternal.

Coloring book

Note

____

____

____

Note